STUDENT BOOK **3**

SERIES EDITORS
Joan Kang Shin & JoAnn (Jodi) Crandall

AUTHORS
Jill Korey O'Sullivan & Joan Kang Shin

Australia • Brazil • Japan • Korea • Mexico • Singapore • Spain • United Kingdom • United States

Let's Share!

I need the paint.

I need the paint, too!

I'm sorry!

That's OK.

3

1 Stand Up, Sit Down

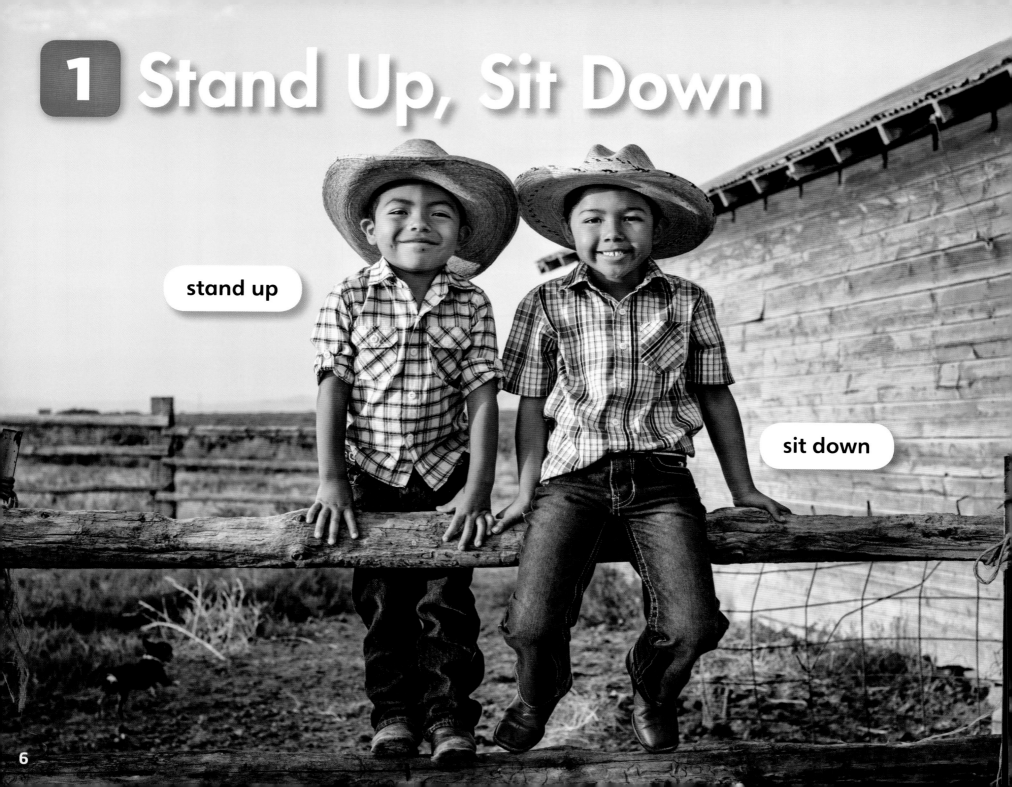

stand up

sit down

touch

read

count

write

draw

color

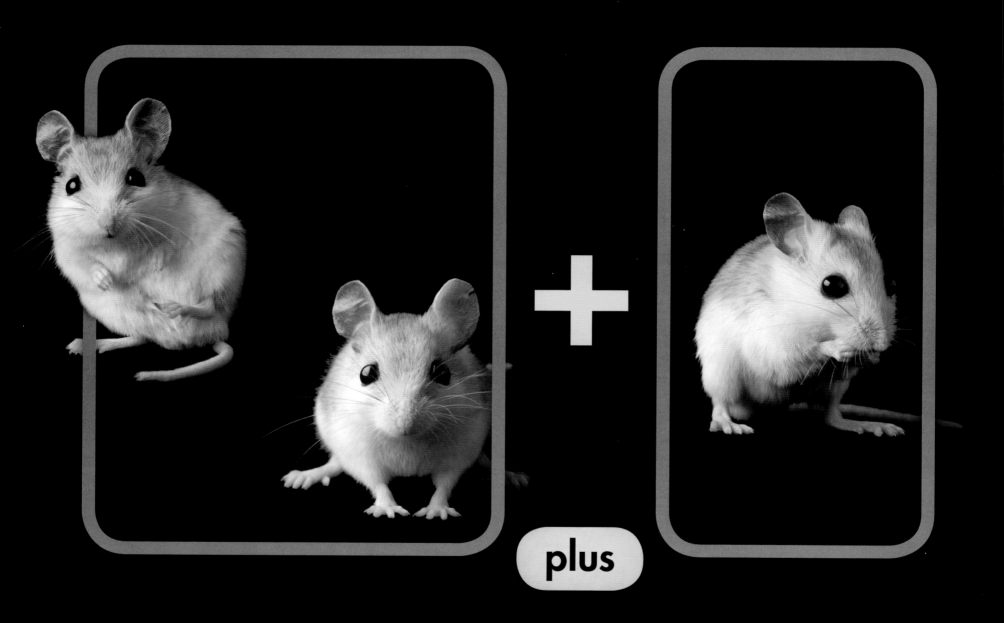

plus

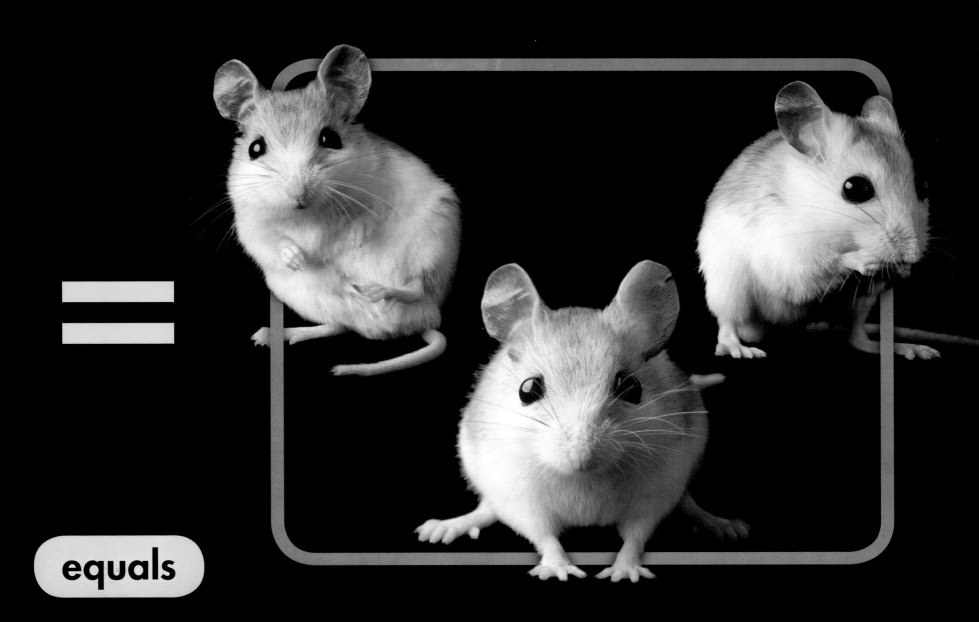

equals

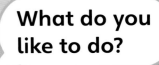
What do you like to do?

I like to draw.

2 It's Raining

an umbrella

raining

windy

cloudy

sunglasses

sunny

snowing

mittens

dry

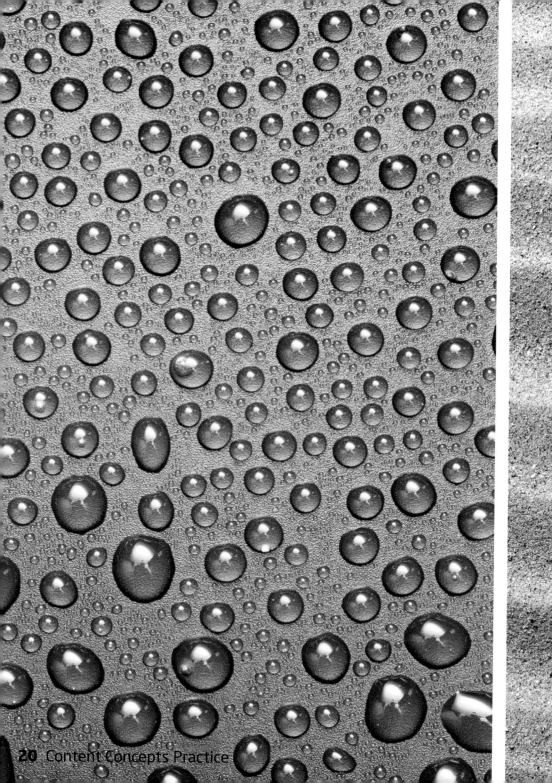

What's the weather like?

It's windy!

3 Wild Animals

a monkey

a penguin

a zebra

an elephant

a tiger

a lion

a frog

a panda

bigger

4 Singing and Dancing

singing

clapping

stomping

a drum

a guitar

dancing

shouting

a piano

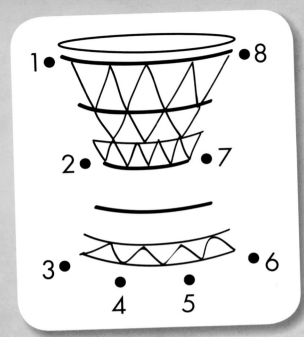

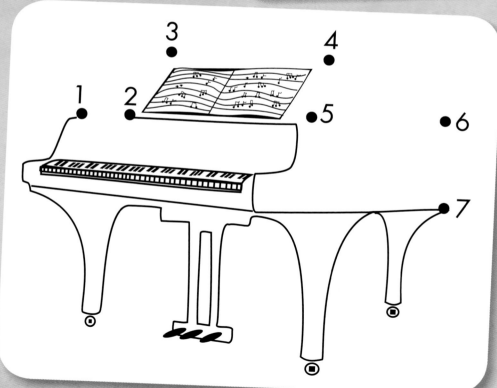

Song **33**

loud

quiet

5 See, Smell, Hear

eat

see

smell

feel

drink

hear

taste

soft

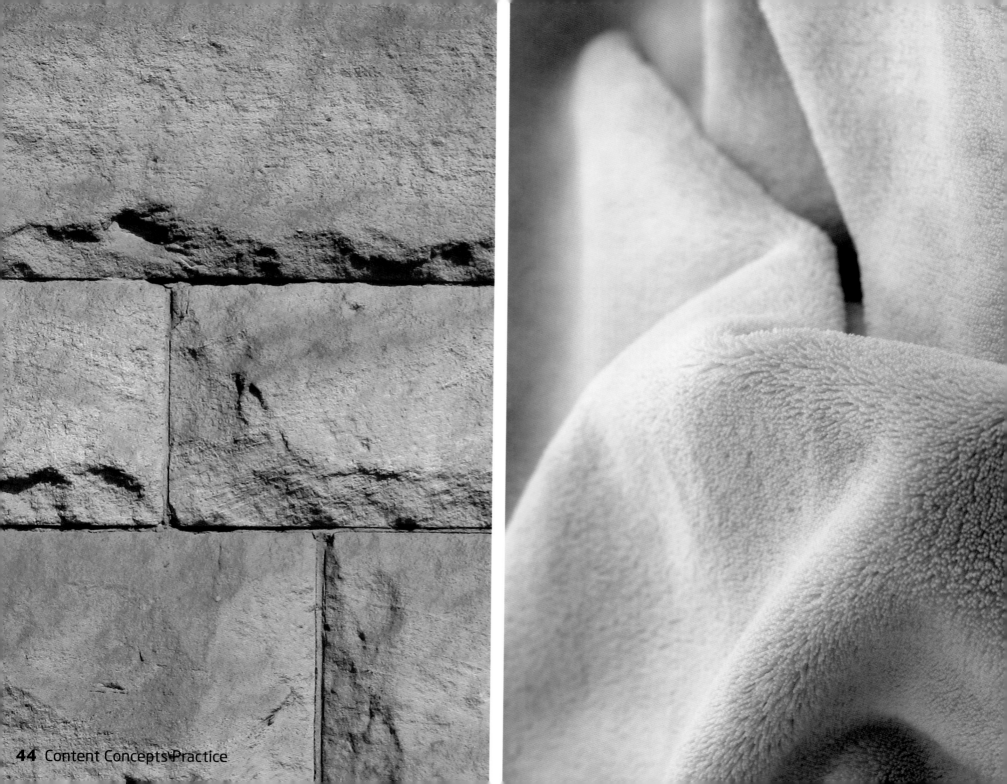

What do you see?

I see a crayon.

6 Story Time

a castle

a king

a queen

a princess

a knight

a dragon

a giant

a treasure

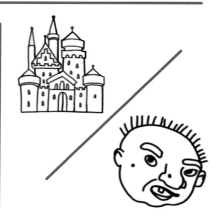

beginning

middle

end

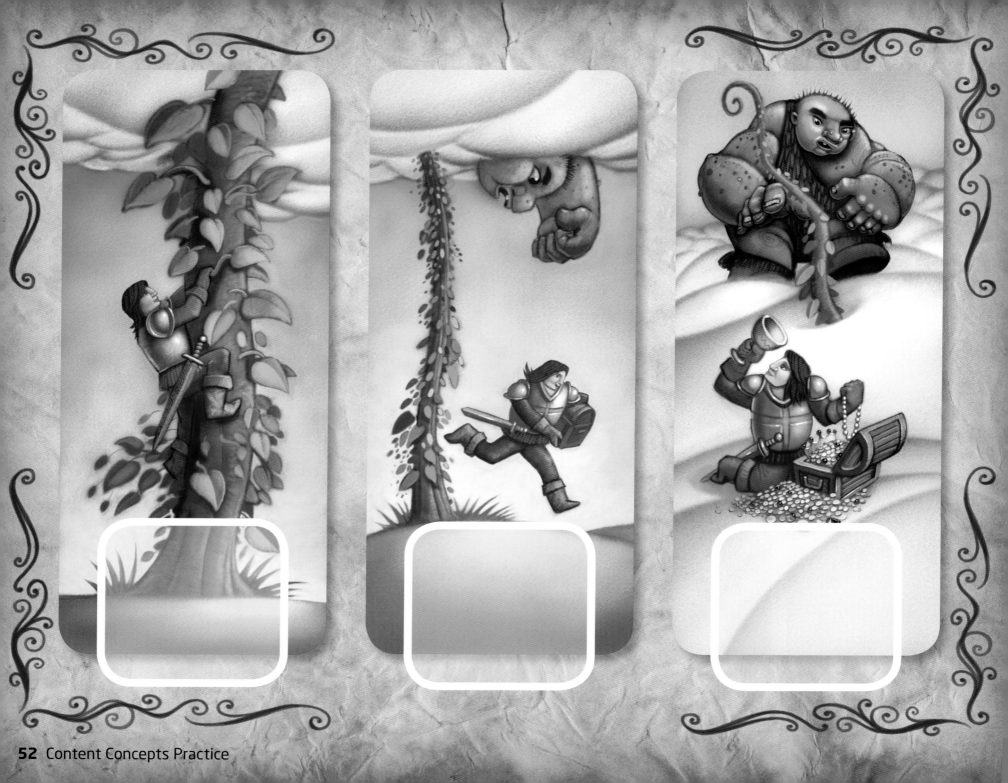

7 It's a Party!

candles

a cake

ice cream

a balloon

pizza

a present

candy

more

less

8 Our World

a cloud

a mountain

a bridge

the sky

the ocean

a river

a road

the world

a city

a country

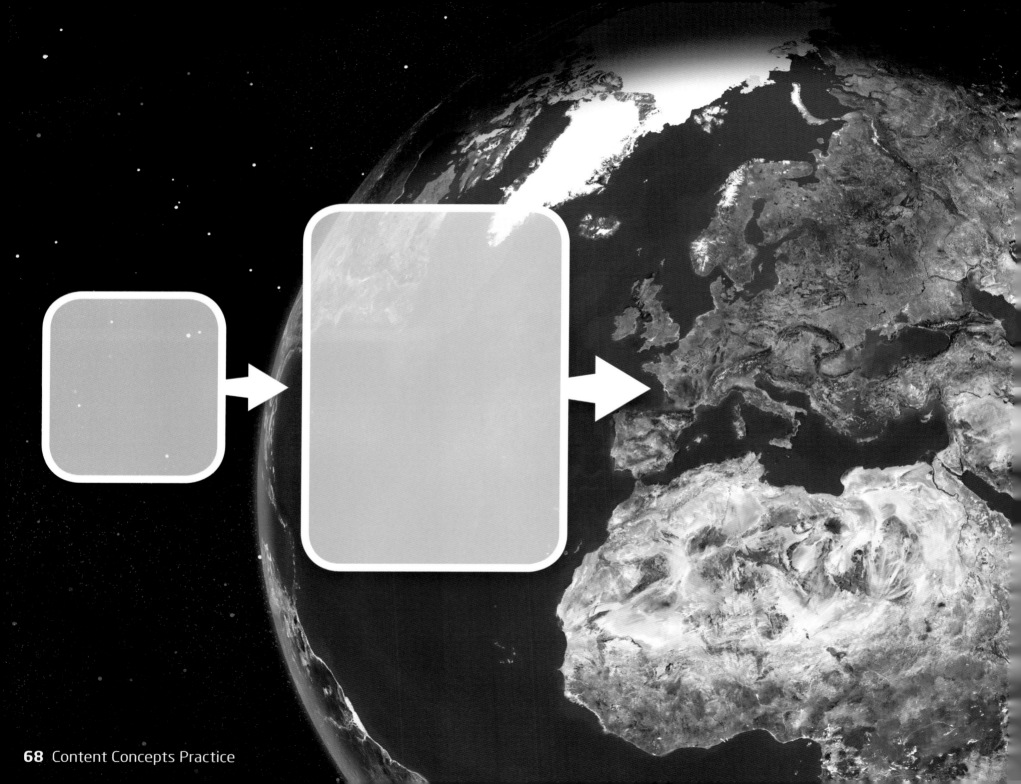

1 Make a counting spider.

2 Make a rainy day scene.

3 Make a penguin.

4 Make a drum.

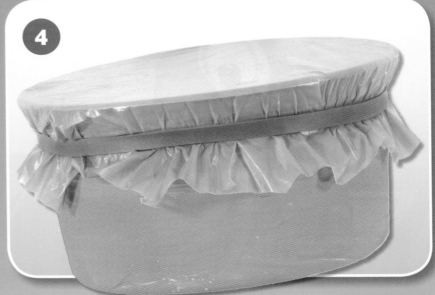

5 Make a five-senses poster.

6 Make a dragon.

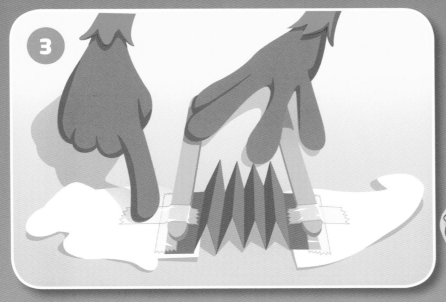

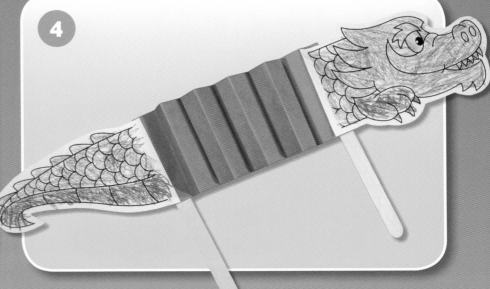

7 Make a pizza.

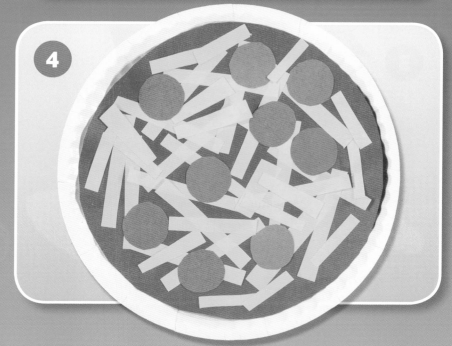

8 Make a globe.

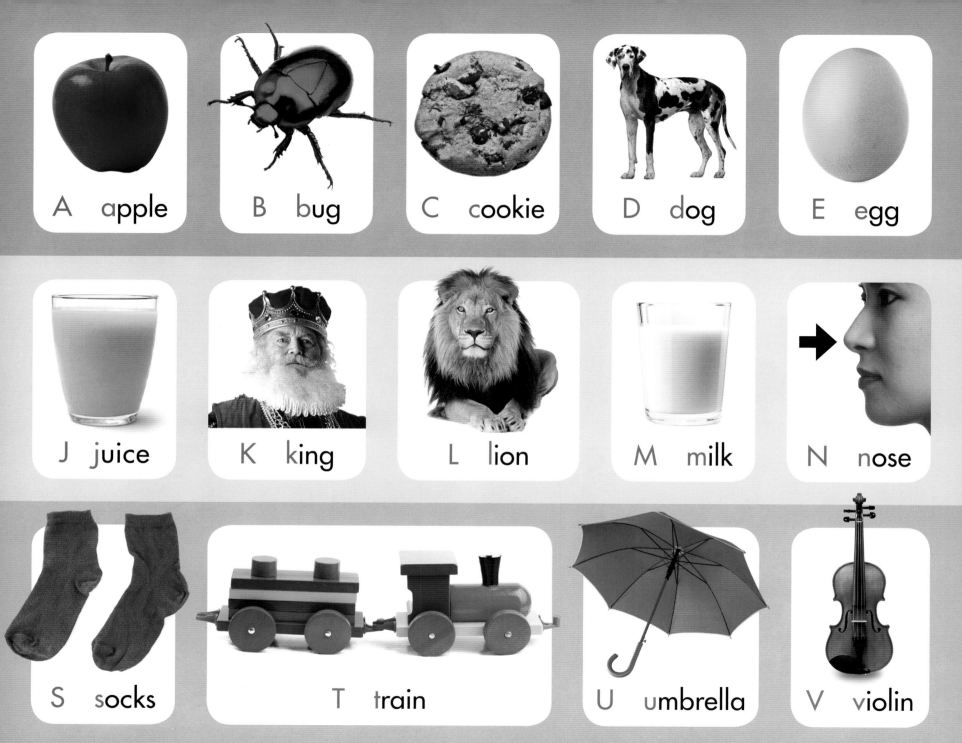

A apple

B bug

C cookie

D dog

E egg

J juice

K king

L lion

M milk

N nose

S socks

T train

U umbrella

V violin

F fire truck

G goat

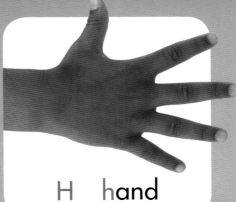

H hand

I ice cream

O orange

P puzzle

Q queen

R rabbit

W window

box X

Y yogurt

Z zebra

1 I can talk about things I do in class.

2 I can talk about the weather.

3 I can talk about wild animals.

4 I can talk about music.

5 I can talk about the senses.

6 I can talk about stories.

7 I can talk about parties.

8 I can talk about my world.